THE RELUCTANT FUNDAMENTALIST

Mira Nair is the rare, prolific filmmaker who fluidly moves between Hollywood and independent cinema. After several years of making documentary films, Mira Nair made a stunning entry on the world stage with her first feature, *Salaam Bombay!* (1988), now hailed as a classic. It was the first Indian film to win the coveted Camera D'Or at the Cannes Film Festival in 1988, followed by more than twenty-five international awards including an Academy Award nomination for Best Foreign Film at the Oscars in 1989. Nair then directed *Mississippi Masala* (1991), *The Perez Family* (1995), *Kama Sutra: A Tale of Love* (1996) and *My Own Country* (1998). In 2001, Nair's *Monsoon Wedding* won the Golden Lion, Venice's top prize in cinema, becoming one of the highest grossing foreign films of all time. Her film for HBO, *Hysterical Blindness* (2002), gave Uma Thurman a Golden Globe for Best Actress, and Emmy Awards for Ben Gazzara and Gena Rowlands. Nair made Thackeray's *Vanity Fair* (2004), followed by the acclaimed adaptation of Jhumpa Lahiri's *The Namesake* (2006), starring Irrfan Khan and Tabu. In 2009, she directed the aviation epic, *Amelia*.

In 2012 Mira Nair was awarded the Padma Bhushan, India's distinguished honour for work in the arts. Her most recent film is *The Reluctant Fundamentalist* (2013) based on the novel by Mohsin Hamid. She is currently involved in the production of the stage musical of her film, *Monsoon Wedding*, due to open on Broadway in 2014.

Nair is a gardener and lives in New Delhi, Kampala and New York City with her husband and son.

THE RELUCTANT FUNDAMENTALIST

FROM BOOK TO FILM

MIRA NAIR

PORTRAIT PHOTOGRAPHY BY BRIGITTE LACOMBE
ON SET PHOTOGRAPHY (INDIA) BY ISHAAN NAIR
ON SET PHOTOGRAPHY (USA) BY QUANTRELL COLBERT

PENGUIN
STUDIO

PENGUIN STUDIO

Published by the Penguin Group

Penguin Books India Pvt. Ltd, 11 Community Centre, Panchsheel Park, New Delhi 110 017, India

Penguin Group (USA) Inc., 375 Hudson Street, New York, New York 10014, USA

Penguin Group (Canada), 90 Eglinton Avenue East, Suite 700, Toronto, Ontario, M4P 2Y3, Canada (a division of Pearson Penguin Canada Inc.)

Penguin Books Ltd, 80 Strand, London WC2R 0RL, England

Penguin Ireland, 25 St Stephen's Green, Dublin 2, Ireland (a division of Penguin Books Ltd)

Penguin Group (Australia), 707 Collins Street, Melbourne, Victoria 3008, Australia (a division of Pearson Australia Group Pty Ltd)

Penguin Group (NZ), 67 Apollo Drive, Rosedale, Auckland 0632, New Zealand (a division of Pearson New Zealand Ltd)

Penguin Books (South Africa) (Pty) Ltd, Block D, Rosebank Office Park, 181 Jan Smuts Avenue, Parktown North, Johannesburg 2193, South Africa

Penguin Books Ltd, Registered Offices: 80 Strand, London WC2R 0RL, England

First published in Penguin Studio by Penguin Books India 2013

Brigitte Lacombe images courtesy of Doha Film Institute
Excerpts from the documentary film *The Global Landscape: Making The Reluctant Fundamentalist* by Marian Lacombe
Poster on page 172 by Akshar Pathak
The Reluctant Fundamentalist logo and Urdu calligraphy on page 178 by Design Temple

ISBN 9780143420620

Book design by Pallavi Agarwala
Printed at Thomson Press Pvt. Ltd, New Delhi

ALWAYS LEARNING   **PEARSON**

CONTENTS

'In the ten years between 9/11 and the killing of Osama Bin Laden, a young man grows up. This is the story of that young man.'
MIRA NAIR

FOREWORD

I believe I may have been put on this earth to tell stories of living between worlds.

My father grew up in Lahore before the partition of India and Pakistan in 1947. As a child of modern India, I was raised like a Lahori—speaking Urdu, quoting the poems of Faiz Ahmed Faiz, listening to the ghazals of Iqbal Bano and Noor Jehan—yet there was a wall between our countries that could never be crossed. It was only in 2004, when I was invited to show my films in Pakistan, that I had the chance to visit the land my father loved, to discover that the country, the culture, the people all seemed heartbreakingly familiar. I was immediately inspired to make a contemporary film about Pakistan, especially in this day and age when the schism between official America and Muslim people becomes more pronounced with each passing day. The great gift came in the form of Mohsin Hamid's elegant mind game of a novel *The Reluctant Fundamentalist*, the enigmatic coming-of-age story of Changez, a young man in Lahore who loves America, achieves the American dream and then, as the world changes around him, begins to question his place in it.

A story about how we, East and West, regard each other.

Over the last few years, we have seen many films about the Iraq and Afghanistan wars, but always told from the American point of view. We have seen noble films of soldiers who return home in body bags, but we will never know the name of the Iraqi woman who has lost her family and her home in the name of freedom and democracy. In this film, the encounter between the characters of Changez and Bobby mirrors the mutual suspicion with which America and Pakistan (or the Muslim world) look at one another. We learn that, as a result of America's war on terror, Changez experiences a seismic shift in his own attitude, unearthing allegiances more fundamental than money, power and maybe even love. But other forms of fundamentalism are revealed along the way, including the kind practiced by Changez's former employer, Underwood Samson. Their model for global expansion is 'Focus on the fundamentals'. From the title of the film, and from the increasingly tense atmosphere arising between Changez and his American listener, the expectation is that Changez is moving towards the revelation that he has gone, however 'reluctantly', all the way over to the dark side of extremism. But is this really the case?

In adapting the story for the screen, *The Reluctant Fundamentalist* became a human thriller, an unflinching dialogue about identity and perception and issues around the divided self in the era of globalization.

When electing to make a film, a film-maker chooses to inhabit a world in which she or he wants to be immersed. For me, one of the joys of making *The Reluctant Fundamentalist* was revealing Pakistan in a way that one never sees it in the newspapers, with its extraordinary refinement, the searing poetry of Faiz, its heart-stopping Sufi music and ancient culture that is confident in fashion, painting and performance. This world is fluidly juxtaposed with the energy of New York, the ruthlessness of corporate America and, through our hero Changez's love for the elegant, artistic Erica, reveals a portrait of Manhattan society at the same exalted level once occupied by Changez's own family back in Lahore.

In the bones of Mohsin's tale, I saw a dialogue between one side and the other. And it is this dialogue that embodies my own life story. I came from India to America when I was nineteen and, like Mohsin, have lived more than half my life outside the subcontinent. Unwittingly, my films, my work and life came to be about the seesaw between these worlds, in which I felt both an insider and an outsider. And like many of us who live hybrid lives, I railed against the line that was drawn a decade ago when Bush coined the 'axis of evil' and built a wall of myopia between one way of life and another.

If we don't tell our own stories, no one else will—that is the mantra by which I live. *The Reluctant Fundamentalist* gave me the chance to create multilayered characters, to move things out of the hot-blooded political debate and into the human, emotional dimension, to see beyond the terrible stereotype that is constantly projected on our television screens and, if we have done our work right, to create a bridge between worlds that will not know each other unless we have a dialogue.

There is one film that has inspired me for decades—the only film in the world I wished I had directed—a path-breaking film that taught me to show both sides of a conflict with equal intelligence, pain and love. This is Gillo Pontecorvo's great classic about the fight for Algerian independence: *The Battle of Algiers*. I had occasion to meet the great man several times in 1991 when, as director of the Venice Film Festival, he invited me to premiere my second film, *Mississippi Masala*. And so it made my heart skip a beat when, two weeks after finally completing

The Reluctant Fundamentalist in Bombay, my phone rang at home in Kampala and it was Antonio Barbera, the new director of the Venice Film Festival, exultantly asking me if *The Reluctant Fundamentalist* could open the festival. The honour was great, the pressure even greater, but of course I said 'YES!' and off we went, a caravan of us, film-makers from four continents, and me secretly praying that the time had come for the Western world to hear of a post 9/11 tale from the 'other' side.

As the hot August night descended on the Lido, I, in my faux-Mughal special, joined Kate Hudson in her eye-popping meshmetal dress, Mohsin in his sherwani tuxedo and Riz in his rapper duds and, protected by fellow film-makers and family, we walked the red carpet past screaming paparazzi to what I hoped would not be my guillotine. The film played beautifully, punctuated by gasps and laughter and occasional tears—it always gives me sweet pleasure to listen to the fullness of our music, the qawwalis, ghazals and tuppaas on distant shores—and, at last, the lights came upon our motley band and we rose to face a standing audience who just wouldn't stop clapping. My facial muscles ached. Someone clocked it as a twelve-minute ovation, and Mohsin joked, 'Just like a book opening . . .'

It was only later in the tented banquet by the sea, after copious quantities of champagne and passionate words about the film from another guru of cinema, Michael Mann, that I began to breathe easier. In the distance, across the candelabras and tiara-ed gowns, I saw a diminutive older lady slowly make her way towards our table, pausing to ask where she could find the director of the film she had just seen. She came towards me and held both my hands. And then, in her mellifluous Italian accent, she said the most beautiful words I could ever have heard: 'I am Gillo Pontecorvo's widow, and I have come to tell you that Gillo lives in you.'

The film is dedicated to my father, Amrit Nair, who sadly passed away in July 2012, the same month the film was completed. He and my mother taught me to disregard the arbitrary borders that separate us, and inspired me to love the land that we come from. It is also made for our twenty-one-year old son Zohran and other young people like him across the world, to urge them to look beyond what is handed to us as truth and, as they make their way into adulthood, to grapple with the fundamental questions of where we belong, what we stand for, where we matter.

8 January 2013   Mira Nair
Kampala, Uganda

Mohsin Hamid
Il fondamentalista riluttante

Traduzione di Norman Gobetti

'Two men meet, have a conversation. A clock is ticking.
A man's life hangs in the balance. You don't know what will
happen—who will live and who will die. The pace and the rhythm
of the film are laced with suspense, but I'm a person who is full
of an appetite for life and beauty and fun and family and fashion.
In my films, you get taken on that ride too.'
MIRA NAIR

I ask only one thing.
That you please listen
to the whole story.
From the very beginning.
Not just bits and pieces.
Do I have your word?

You do.

ADAPTATION

FROM NOVEL TO SCREENPLAY

Is there a Pakistani dream?

MIRA NAIR

DIRECTOR

Ever since I returned from Lahore that first time in 2004, I looked for a tale to tell of contemporary Pakistan, a tale one never sees. It was while finishing *The Namesake* in New York in 2007 that I read the unpublished manuscript of Mohsin Hamid's novel *The Reluctant Fundamentalist*. I immediately recognized it as the one. Not only did it give me a chance to speak about our subcontinental worlds, but it was equally a dialogue with America. I discussed the matter with Lydia Pilcher, and through our production houses—my own Mirabai Films and Lydia's New York-based Cine Mosaic—we optioned the film rights to the novel.

I knew that this was to be a very complex adaptation and I wanted to be very involved in its shaping. The book is basically a monologue. The thriller element is there, but in a very elegant and psychological way—even the ending is ambiguous. However, this sort of ambiguity would not work as neatly in a film. For instance, the character of the American, played by Liev Schreiber, needed to be fleshed out into a living and breathing character. He had to have an equal intelligence, and as much grace and longing and pain as Changez. I wanted the film to include more of what happens in Pakistan. In many ways, Pakistan is crucial to Changez's story. But this decision was motivated by more personal reasons as well. I wanted to make a contemporary film about Pakistan, one that would break all misconceptions about the country and reveal it in a manner not seen before—as a simmering, confident nation caught between its ancient heritage and the demands of a globalized world.

Meanwhile, finding a writer to accurately render both the world of corporate Wall Street and that of Lahore in South Asia was proving impossible. In fact, talking to writers from all over the world was a very revealing process. One writer even said, 'First off, we're going to have to drop the title. You couldn't drag me to see a film with the word "fundamentalist" in it.' Clearly, there was real ignorance of this part of the world—the subcontinent. There was no knowledge of the cultural layers, of the refinements. It also revealed the myopia with which many people see the world.

Lydia and I looked closer to home for the writer we needed—to the young writer Ami Boghani, who has worked closely with me for years, and to Mohsin Hamid, who had never even read a screenplay before joining the writing team. Mohsin was hesitant at first. He knew that a film is a very different medium from a novel, and he was aware that he was new to this. But he loves movies, was turned on by the collaborative ride we all chose to take, and is one of the most open-minded people I know. His lack of preciousness about his work, his faith in knowing that making a film of his story entailed entrusting it to another medium entirely—this gave us a free and flexible journey for what was to take the better part of five years.

Ami instinctively understood the challenge of fleshing out the part of Changez's story that takes place in Pakistan. In the novel, Mohsin builds a thriller out of two men sitting at a table. Never breaking from the one-sided monologue, Mohsin only hints at the context in which these two men are meeting. Our major task in the film adaptation was fully developing that context by answering the key question, 'Why is Changez telling his story?' We had to translate the dance of mutual suspicion into visual language by fleshing out the two men sitting at that table and understanding how they got there.

Two drafts of the screenplay were written over two and a half years. Together, we put much of the script's foundation in place: Changez's family, his relationship with his father, the tone of the film and the examination of the two fundamentals of money and religion.

But what we found was that writing a thriller was not an easy thing. We needed someone more adept at that. And so we found William Wheeler through a screenplay we all admired. The four of us spent a week together and mapped out Changez's journey within the flow of the film's narrative. Bill then wrote a series of drafts, and gradually everything fell into place.

RIOT SCENE — STORYBOARDS
20/11

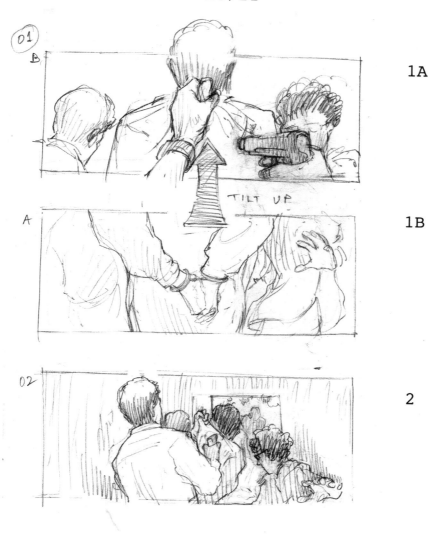

01

B

1A

TILT UP

A

1B

02

2

RIOT SCENE — STORYBOARDS
20/11

3

4

5

RIOT SCENE — STORYBOARDS
20/11

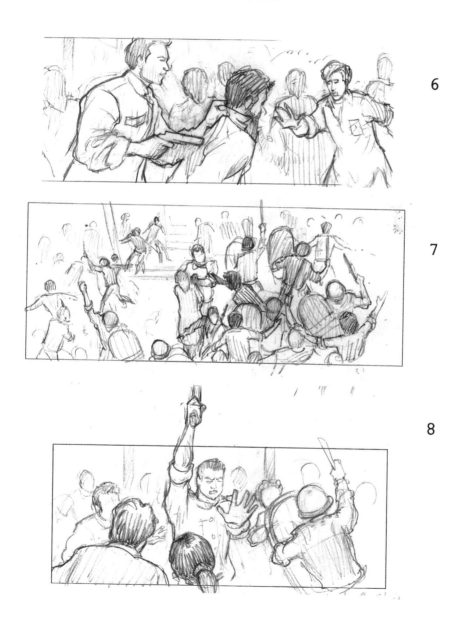

6

7

8

RIOT SCENE — STORYBOARDS
20/11

9

SAMEER HIT BY BULLET

10

11

RIOT SCENE — STORYBOARDS
20/11

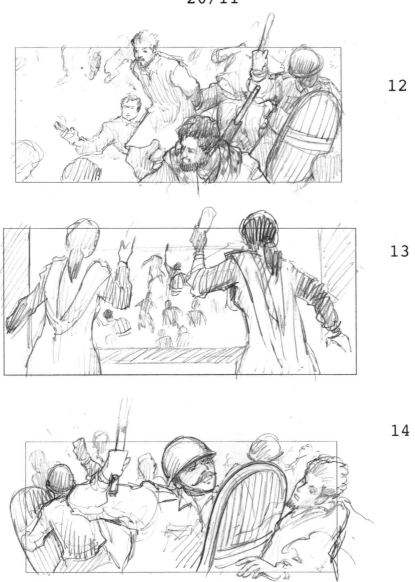

12

13

14

INT. PAK TEA HOUSE, STAIRS - CONTINUOUS

Bobby leads Changez down the staircase towards the exit,
Junaid, Sameer, and some others jostling around them. The
students outside have surrounded the building.

> CHANGEZ
> You're going to get us both killed,
> Bobby.

He raises his voice and commands his students in Urdo.

> CHANGEZ (CONT'D)
> Everyone step back!

Words aren't enough for Bobby, who fires a single shot into
the air. The frenzy increases.

> BOBBY
> He's in a freezer! A butcher's
> freezer!

> CHANGEZ
> You're making a mistake that will
> get us both killed!

One aggressive student JUMPS at Bobby. As Bobby falls to the
dusty floor, his gun FIRES.

EXT. PAK TEA HOUSE - MOMENTS LATER

Knocked over, Changez blinks at the sound of a SHRIEKING
WOMAN somewhere in the plaza. She wails because she kneels
over the fallen body of

Sameer.

The accidental shot from Bobby's pistol has struck Sameer in
the torso. His face moves for a moment, and then is still.

EXT. PAK TEA HOUSE, ON THE STREET - MOMENTS LATER

In an attempt to escape from the gun battle - the students
and pedestrians on the street THROW themselves against the
riot shields of the Lahore police. Fearing an escalation,
Lahore Police baton strike repeatedly on protestors' hands
and heads...

> COOPER (O.S.)
> Move!   Move!

INT. SUV, IN THE DRIVER'S SEAT, LAHORE - DAY

In the driver's seat of the SUV, Cooper barks orders into a headset. The SUV is in an archway, SURROUNDED by furious students, POUNDING its doors.

                    COOPER
          Just secure Bobby and get the hell
          back here. Go!

Three AMERICAN GUNMEN push out from the back seat. Two wave M-5 machine pistols. The crowd PULLS BACK from sight of the weapons. A thin path opens up to the cafe.

The sound of GUNNING ENGINES outside. Several BMW SUVS roar up to the entrance of the cafe.

EXT. PAK TEA HOUSE - DAY

Changez has rushed to the side of Sameer.

He has removed the young man's shirt and begun administering CPR. A medical student from the university assists him.

Backing toward the front entrance, Bobby waves his gun at the six or seven students that have spotted him and identified him as the shooter.

Bobby SHOOTS his GUN in the air, hoping to back them off.

The furious patrons throw rocks and coffee mugs at Bobby, as they wait for cover to approach him.

Junaid waves his hands at the men coming in.

                    JUNAID
              (subtitled, in Urdu)
          No firing!   No firing!

RIOT SCENE — STORYBOARDS
20/11

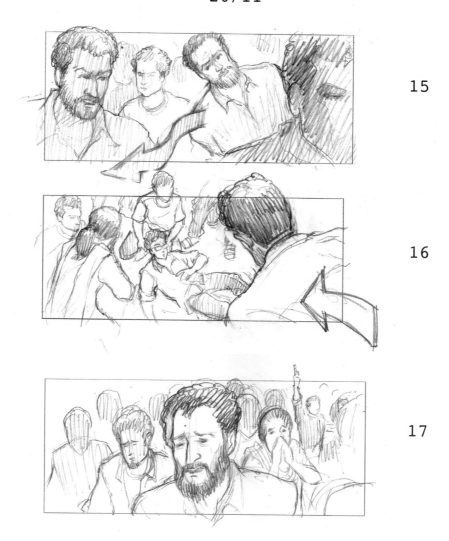

15

16

17

AMI BOGHANI

SCREEN STORY WRITER AND CO-PRODUCER

Here it is. You must read it right away., Mira Nair plunked her dog-eared copy of *The Reluctant Fundamentalist* on my desk. Her energy was focused, her tone buoyant. In the five years I'd worked with her, I had come to understand that this meant she was creatively hooked and raring to go. Now it was time for the rest of her team to catch up.

From my very first read, I was captured by the cleanness and beauty of Mohsin Hamid's prose, the way he painted his beloved Lahore with precise strokes of light and shadow. But I found the novel's true genius in the way Mohsin managed to weave Changez's monologue into a political thriller. He turns a linear narrative structure on its head, guiding his readers along an emotional mobius strip until we are left facing ourselves, questioning our own perceptions. Needless to say, I finished the book in a single sitting, inspired but also baffled. I thought, how on earth is this going to be adapted into a screenplay?

The key was to translate the experience of reading Mohsin's novel into a visual medium. Mira and her producing partner, Lydia Pilcher, led the charge, with interviews and writing samples, research and brainstorm sessions, timelines and newspaper clippings, treatments and pitches. As a comparative rookie in the development game, I found it fascinating to work alongside these seasoned pros to put the puzzle pieces together. Working with Mohsin himself and LA-based screenwriter William Wheeler, we synthesized all of the weapons in our collective mental arsenal to extract a powerful, fast-paced screen story from the novel,s contemplative monologue, all the while manoeuvering to keep the essence of the story intact.

Meanwhile, Pakistan's own history was being written in front of our very eyes. While the screenplay was in development, President Musharraf declared a state of emergency and started sacking Supreme Court Justices; Benazir Bhutto was killed in Rawalpindi and Asif Ali Zardari, her widower, came to power; Raymond Davis, an American CIA contractor, gunned down civilians in Lahore; and six months before production began, Osama bin Laden was found and killed in Abbottabad. Mira tasked the writing team with keeping the film utterly contemporary yet resoundingly timeless and so, as the landscape of Pakistan changed, our screenplay evolved alongside it.

I see the film as a true testament to both the power of artistic vision and unrelenting perseverance. From those writing sessions in London, Lahore, and New York to financing meetings in Doha to production in Atlanta, Delhi, and Istanbul to post-production in Mumbai and on to sparkling red carpets in Venice and Toronto, it has been an incredible journey. I'm honoured to be part of the team that made *The Reluctant Fundamentalist* a reality.

WILLIAM WHEELER
CO-SCREENWRITER

While I enjoy very much novels and plays that are highly ambiguous—the work of Pinter comes to mind—I didn't think the ambiguity of the novel could sustain a cinematic narrative. Yet the success of Mohsin's novel is very intertwined with this frame narrative, specifically the intrigue and menace of the implied confrontation between the two men. Who was the unnamed American? Was he an intelligence agent? Was he meeting Changez with the intent to turn him? Capture him? And what about Changez? Did the American have reason to fear him? Could it be that the modality Changez had 'reluctantly' embraced was a political approach that included violence? These questions swam in my head while reading the novel, fascinating me and pulling me in, and I wanted the audience asking these same questions.

This ongoing sense of mystery around Changez's ultimate disposition—the nature of his reaction to the xenophobia that enveloped him in 2001—was an element I was determined not to lose in the film.

In a collaborative process, the writing team decided that like the novel, the story would shift between two timeframes, but, unlike the novel, the present-day story would be a fully fleshed out espionage story with a beginning, a middle and an end. This required the invention of several new elements: the kidnapping of Anse Rainier, the presence of an American intelligence unit in Lahore and, most importantly, the character of Bobby Lincoln—the cinematic equivalent of the unnamed American in Mohsin's novel.

Giving Bobby just and reasonable arguments for the US presence in Pakistan while at the same time maintaining the power of Changez's critique of that presence—in addition to his experience in Underwood Samson and the United States overall—would, we hoped, allow members of the audience to engage with the material through their own individual perspectives. Working with partners from such varied cultural backgrounds made our collaboration an attempt, like that of Changez and Bobby, to reach across cultural divides to try and discover the things that make us all human.

MOHSIN HAMID

NOVELIST AND SCREEN STORY WRITER

Mira profoundly and intuitively understood my novel, so I was confident about her being at the helm of affairs. I really clicked with her as a person too. She is someone who comes from South Asia and has spent many years here but has lived abroad for almost half her life. I am the same.

When I was first invited to help with the screenplay, I was hesitant—partly because I was writing my novel; partly because I thought this was Mira's film. I wanted to enjoy it as a well-wisher but I didn't want to get into the conflicts that I thought would be inevitable if we had to argue out the details of how things should work. But then I kept telling myself the film is inspired by the novel, but it isn't the novel on screen. Once I embraced that way of looking at things, it became much easier to become involved. I also thought it would be a good learning experience. I would become more familiar with this art form about which I know very little.

I recall Mira telling me early on that she was going to add a third act to the story of my novel. She wanted to have more of what happens in Pakistan. My novel primarily deals with the character of Changez going to America and then coming back to Pakistan. This part of Changez's story needed to be fleshed out, including the circumstances that lead to his conversation with the American. This addition was the first significant departure from my novel. But my main sense was that Mira is a film-maker and knows what she is doing. If a film—her film—needed to be this way I was going to trust her on that.

As a novelist, I found it fascinating to watch a film being made. In many ways, Mira does what I do as a novelist—construct and painstakingly craft a story. But she also does things I don't have to, like marshall 230 people for weeks on end. What I can do in a sentence or a paragraph, she has to build an entire set to do, and she needs carpenters, electricians and painters to do it. I operate in a pleasant little cocoon, just me and my computer, quietly working away. She has to create this beautiful, impactful thing in complete chaos, with phones ringing, last-minute problems developing, traffic violations, electricity shortages—all kinds of crazy stuff. I am much more appreciative now of how difficult it is to make a good film.

THE RELUCTANT FINANCIER

LYDIA DEAN PILCHER

PRODUCER

The films Mira and I make together are inevitably undertaken with a fierce independent spirit and a twist of subversiveness. Mohsin Hamid's novel *The Reluctant Fundamentalist* offered us an opportunity to honestly explore many of the political themes that besiege our world when East meets West and commerce clashes with culture. It was an ambitious prospect and, as an American producing *The Reluctant Fundamentalist*, I was constantly presented with unusual challenges.

After coming out on top in a bidding war for the book rights, we entered a long thoughtful period of script development. Mohsin Hamid was eager to work with us to find ways to take his literary psychological thriller into a realm of commercial, albeit provocative, entertainment. Narrative invention was required in the adaptation, although we always found ourselves coming back to the basic structure of the novel and Changez's personal story. Mira was drawn to the deeper cultural layers of the worlds in the story as well. Changez addressing his university class—'Is there a Pakistani dream? . . . One that doesn't involve emigrating?'—speaks to Mira's desire to celebrate the richness of Pakistani culture, music and traditions that are often left behind by the Western media, but cannot be left behind in one's soul and personal identity.

By the fall of 2010 we had a screenplay, thanks to development finance and support from Hani Farsi of Corniche Pictures in London, and we began to cast the movie and reach out to potential partners. I met with numerous financiers, distributors and sales agents, who were very interested and very curious to track the casting process. At the Doha Tribeca Film Festival in Qatar we met with the Doha Film Institute, who loved the project and committed to providing the first cornerstone of equity.

I was soon to learn, however, that it was going to be a challenge to finance a film whose beating heart is the complicated character of Changez. As I continued to look for partners, a British financier of award-winning films pressured me to lower the budget. I told him it was very difficult to reduce costs without sacrificing the global scope. His response was, 'I don't care if you shoot in Rockaway Beach darling, let's face it, your leading man is a Pakistani Muslim.' In a business where world sales estimates set the stage, we were fighting an uphill battle in terms of commercial risk. Ultimately, Mira and I forensically parsed down the budget, taking decisions such as shooting digitally and saving around $1 million by doing the post-production work in India.

Another hurdle was the inclination of European financiers to view the political conflicts of the story as an 'American' problem rather than part of a global dynamic. Much of Changez's resentment towards America is fuelled by the feeling of America's self-serving presence in Pakistan, the powerlessness of the people and their dependence on American support as a cause for shame.

To be honest, living in Tribeca during 9/11, I was always unnerved by how many people around me were asking, 'How could this happen?' The question itself seemed to suggest a lack of awareness of the deep, fraught perceptions of our country abroad. It seemed that conflict invited people to take sides, to revert to fundamental beliefs. On one of our early location scouting trips to Atlanta, upon hearing the title of the movie, a main asked me if we were going to be filming in a lot of churches. The disconnects, the ironies, the parallels. My work in terms of how to talk about the movie was cut out for me: to banner the international relevance in the foreign sales marketplace and to appeal to democratic sensibilities domestically.

In pitching the project to financiers and buyers, the big themes were always very clear: two worlds coming together to have a dialogue, cultures living within other cultures, bias and identity and the divided self. To drive home the relevance of the film, we also foregrounded the theme of globalization and the predatory capitalist economics that were manifested in Changez's job on Wall Street. I personally was moved by the part of the novel when Changez begins to travel outside of America in his work as a financial analyst, and his view of the world takes a turn. He comments on the prodigious changes in the eastern part of the globe, 'I felt like a distance runner who thinks he is not doing too badly until he glances over his shoulder and sees that the fellow who is lapping him is not the leader of the pack, but one of the laggards.'

I've produced with international partners for twenty years and share the daily experience of how technology and digital culture crosses borders, knocks down walls and continues to rapidly change the way we communicate, do business and navigate a new world economy. The sheer scope and pace of these changes is staggering. The idea of economic fundamentalism was a theme that appealed to us and the international sales market as well.

As we assembled our cast, we found that many people felt personally committed to the ideas of the film and wanted to leverage their star power in making sure the movie went forward. This was certainly true with the actors Riz Ahmed, Kate Hudson, Kiefer Sutherland, Shabana Azmi, Om Puri and Liev Schreiber. And they were excited to work with Mira, whose irrepressible zest for life and eye for beauty and texture prevail even when plumbing the most visceral, and often frightening, depths of humanity. These actors believed that her lens would tell a story that could be far-reaching. Ultimately, the Doha Film Institute (DFI) believed this as well. They became our major partner, and its founder and chair, Sheikha Mayassa, was a solid supporter with tremendous vision throughout the process.

Our film-making team began to come together—our collective fabric and points of view mirrored the multi-layers of our story. The heads of the creative departments included an Irish-American director of photography, an American composer, an Indian editor, an Indian costume designer, a British production designer, a South African script supervisor and Indian and American sound designers. And we had full-on local crews everywhere we filmed in Istanbul, Delhi, Lahore, Atlanta and New York.

Each city brought its own creative energy to the project. Atlanta, a production choice for tax incentives, was a great stage to create the world of Erica's New York. There was a fascinating dynamism in shooting in the Muslim neighbourhoods of Old Delhi for Lahore, and layering in the exterior textures from a second unit in Pakistan. And finally, although changing the locale of the publishing company—from Chile in the novel to Istanbul in the film—was born out of a need to minimize production costs, the choice of Istanbul was very significant. Istanbul is a transcontinental city where East meets West, with a commercial and historical centre situated in Europe, while one third of its population lives in Asia. The Chilean publisher in the novel tells Changez a story about the jannisaries and, serendipitously, we found ourselves filming a Turkish publisher in the very homeland of the ancient Ottoman Empire.

Everywhere we travelled and filmed the people who joined the crew to become part of the team did so because they felt this was a rare opportunity to be part of a film that voices a point of view outside of the mainstream. This story, as told from Changez's point of view, is unusual for a movie of this size and scope, and people were interested in staking a claim in a dialogue for a new common ground.

When I'm away from home, I'm often reminded that the world doesn't view America the way America views itself. Our team collaborated and furthered Mira's and Mohsin's vision of presenting complexity, without trying to reach simplistic judgments or reductive resolutions. I was heartened to read a review of our world premiere in Venice that stated, 'this is a pro-American film that dares to voice un-American thoughts'. Some say that the shortest distance between two people is a story. Deep in our hearts we all hope that the film will have some impact in shifting our consciousness about the new world economy and the way we live with each other.

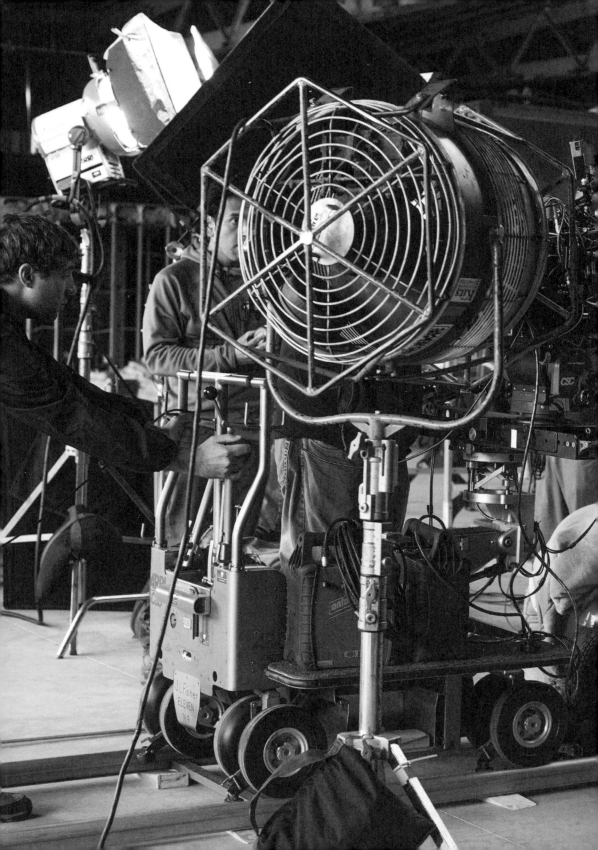

'We haven't seen a character like Changez on film. What this
film gives you is a human being with whom to empathize.
It moves things out of the hot-blooded political debate and
into the emotional, human dimension—and hopefully it does
this well enough to disarm and surprise the audience.'
MOHSIN HAMID

Looks can be deceiving.
I am a lover of America.

In America I get an equal chance to win. And whether you hire me or not, Jim, I am going to win.

Good fucking answer.

You're a long way from Lahore, kid.

I felt I was entering in New York the same social class my family was falling out of in Lahore.

CASTING

MIRA NAIR

DIRECTOR

The most important thing always was casting Changez. It was a very tough role to be able to inhabit with finesse, familiarity and elegance.

The search for an actor to play Changez took around one and a half years and was conducted across several continents. I was counting on a charismatic Pakistani actor—or certainly a subcontinental one—someone who could move fluidly between the languages and disparate worlds with truthful ease and have the skill to carry the movie on his shoulders. I also wanted someone to swoon over—I find the combination of machismo and beauty in Pakistani men quite alluring. But for the longest time, I wasn't able to find the combination I needed of an authentic Pakistani young man who speaks Urdu and who dreams in English, who can be as elegant in a Wall Street corporate party as he is with his family in Lahore.

I remember I had whittled the list down to two actors in Pakistan—one in Lahore, the other in Karachi. However, visas for them were absolutely impossible, which meant I had to visit them there, which was very arduous. Also, we couldn't test them with the actress for Erica in New York. I auditioned charismatic young Bollywood stars, Middle-Easterners of all lands, beautiful boys who did perfume commercials, and scores of young pros in New York and Los Angeles.

The challenges became insurmountable and, by December 2010, while in London en route to Paris on a financing trip, Lydia and I engaged English casting director Susie Figgis, who had cast *Mississippi Masala*. I'd had it with looking for beauty. Intelligence is what I knew I had to have—one cannot direct intelligence. Susie said there was one person: Riz Ahmed, a British actor and rapper who has been gaining a reputation as an articulate and intelligent rising star, thanks to roles in independent films such as *Shifty*, *The Road to Guantanamo* and *Four Lions*. I had only seen *Four Lions* and vaguely remembered seeing audition tapes of him against a green wall.

We called Riz. He was in a studio, in the middle of a recording, but dropped everything and came over. When he arrived, I gave him the scene with his father at the wedding and I said, just read it. It was a cold reading but because of the time he just had to do it. And he did. It was so moving because he understood what Changez had done to his father. He understood shame and he understood honour. Those things are hard to explain. And the role was his immediately.

Riz grasped the challenges that this role presented with an instinctive ease. The entire film pivoted on this character. And, in many ways, Changez personifies the complexity of the film. There is a moment when he stands in a hotel room, watching the destruction of the Twin Towers on television, and describes his first reaction as one of awe. It is a provocative and brave moment in the film. That moment is intended as a very honest description of differences that exist in the world. There are people who had that reaction. The film is not trying to celebrate them or to say that this is good, but it doesn't flinch away from saying, 'This is the way things are.' The challenge is to represent an uneasy reality by locating this feeling inside a character who not only falls in love with an American woman, but also very much falls in love with America itself. Portraying this may be deeply disturbing and off-putting to some people, but we are saying it in a context that isn't polemical. We are simply saying, 'This is the world we live in.'

By no means were the other roles being ignored during all this. Simultaneously, actors were being hired from around the world by New York-based casting director Cindy Tolan, who had worked with me on *The Namesake*. Liaising with casting contacts in Europe, her months of searching spanned North America, India and Pakistan.

Liev Schreiber wanted to meet with me to lobby for the role of Bobby Lincoln, the American in conversation with Changez. We had lunch and I saw he could certainly play Bobby. In fact, he was the first to be cast. I wanted a great parallel between Bobby and Changez—between the American and the Pakistani—so as to make the underlying comment that, if there were another world, these two men would actually be great mates because they are in many ways similar to each other.

I had been impressed by Liev's work on stage in *Talk Radio* and *A View from the Bridge*. He is deeply charismatic, with an amazing voice. He has an authority and a stature that raises the bar on everything. He had also lived in India for some years in his youth. That was good for me—he's like a worldly hippie.

Kiefer Sutherland was the next to board the project. He was perfect for the role of Jim Cross, the managing director of a fictional high-end boutique Wall Street hedge fund called

Underwood Samson. Jim hires Changez and becomes a father figure of sorts to the young Pakistani man as he initially thrives in this meritocratic environment.

Kiefer was passionate about our screenplay and immediately committed himself to the project. Jim is a three-dimensional, complex person, not a cipher for everything wrong with the Western world's financial system. He represents many positives about Western society, particularly the clear-sighted way in which he sees Changez. Jim is the best of America. He comes from the America where somebody like Changez can come in with the wrong skin colour and wrong last name at the trickiest of times and still be treated brilliantly because of his mind.

I have used the world of Underwood Samson to explore the concept of economic fundamentalism alongside that of political fundamentalism. The film suggests there are many belief systems, based on their own fundamentals, that ignore the views and fate of those people who do not share their opinion. The world of finance, the film implies, is based on the notion of profit at all costs—a notion where the end always justifies the means. This is exemplified by Jim's and Changez's ruthless rationalization of companies, which results in hundreds of faceless employees losing their jobs and their livelihoods.

While at Underwood Samson, Changez meets and falls in love with Erica, a young and enigmatic artist. The relationship between Erica and Changez develops through the tragedy of 9/11, and we see the impact on them, as well as on the city itself.

It was wonderful happenstance that Kate Hudson played the role of Erica. Her agents kept insisting we had to meet—I had loved her effervescence in *Almost Famous*, and her six minutes on screen with Daniel Day Lewis in *Nine* were worth the price of admission; but was she Erica? It was in early 2011 that I rang the doorbell to her wonderfully rambling old Hollywood home filled with extraordinary Indian artefacts—and was surprised to find her eight months' pregnant. We both looked at each other at the door, her shapely stomach between us, and began to laugh. This was something the agents had forgotten to mention. It was wordlessly clear she couldn't shoot in a month—we both were sure of that, so we happily curled up on her couch for the next two hours and chatted, which is something I rarely do. We parted ways, promising to work together some day and I went off to other meetings with other actresses— but without falling in love. I went to Delhi to begin prepping the movie and Kate kept sending me love notes as her baby came into the world. And then lo and behold, one of our investors disappeared a few weeks before the shoot so we had to shut down. We began again two months later, which meant that Kate could do the movie after all! It was meant to be. By then I had also cast Riz.

I couldn't film a female character I didn't want to be with. I wasn't arrested by the novel's Erica. For the film, we reconceived Erica as a struggling artist, made more complicated by the privilege she has been born into, and wounded by a secret in her past. She is immersed in herself, yet porous about the world around her, so much so that she doesn't see where art ends and exploitation begins. As with Jim, the duality in Erica is what makes her character recognizably real. She embodies elements of an artistic, bohemian, aspirational, American way of life. But, of course, life and love and people are not simple. And just as America ultimately betrays Changez, so too does Erica—though unwittingly—when her Brechtian political art installation has the opposite effect on Changez than the one she had intended.

Then there was Changez's family in Pakistan. I finally got to work with two friends of mine whom I have admired for decades: the legendary Indian star Om Puri plays Changez's father, a poet steeped in the traditions of rich Lahori culture, and Shabana Azmi, the acclaimed Indian actress—who, like Changez, comes from an esteemed literary and theatre family—plays Changez's mother. Changez's parents embody the elegance and soul of upper-middle-class contemporary Lahoris, living and surviving in a country that deals with the pressure of constant economic and political challenges. Keeping them on their feet is their daughter Bina, a lively young woman who represents the multifaceted modern Pakistani woman. Bina's role was played by the glamorous and hugely talented Meesha Shafi, whose haunting voice on *Coke Studio Pakistan* had kept me going through the turbulence of developing this film.

One of the significant characters in the story is Nazmi Kemal, a publisher in Istanbul whose cautionary tale about the janissaries serving their adopted empire compels Changez to finally change the direction of his life. One of the great gifts of the film is the performance of Haluk Bilginer, the great Turkish actor, who plays Kemal. In his erudite elegance, he reminded me of Edward Said and Richard Burton, and he was so accomplished and cool that he happily went on our low-budget ride and shot all his scenes in one eighteen-hour day.

RIZ AHMED

CHANGEZ

I kind of stalked this project. When I first read the book, I loved it! I thought it absolutely must be made into a film. I even called the publisher, asking if I could have the film rights. Of course, the proposal was promptly declined.

I forgot about it for a while, until I realized that the film was indeed being made. It wasn't easy to get an audition. And based on what Mira had seen of my work—essentially my left-field choice of roles—she wasn't entirely sure if I could play a romantic lead. Still, I felt I could really play Changez. I had given up all hope until I got the last-minute call to go and see her and we clicked.

Changez is very different from the characters I have previously inhabited in films with broadly similar themes—his personal conflicts are arguably more pronounced. Those other characters I have played confront shifting events that they have to manage. However, for Changez, his entire sense of self shifts. His journey is a deeply personal and psychological one, but it takes place in the context of a thriller—another reason this role appealed to me so strongly.

The film is very bold in that it talks to our need to communicate and be understood. I think this is particularly important in the context of the so-called 'clash of civilizations'. But the film-making experience resonated with me on a personal level rather than a political one. For one, the emotional journey of trying to find home is a universal one we can all relate to. Also, I made an interesting discovery while filming in Old Delhi. We were filming in an old compound called the Anglo-Arabic Islamic School, when I happened to learn my granddad's uncle used to be president of this college. It was a way for me to unexpectedly reconnect with my own heritage as well.

A lot of the film is about Changez trying to find his identity. In a sense, precisely because he's coming from a family of artists and poets, Wall Street is a kind of rebellion for him. His conflicted sense of who he is—his vantage point between classes and cultures—is one that can tell us a very timely story about who we are, who we think we are and what it is that we value.

LIEV SCHREIBER
BOBBY LINCOLN

'To be honest, what initially attracted me to the project was Mira. She was someone I admired and was eager to work with, on anything. Then I read Mohsin's book and I felt it was a really timely piece, and provocative in a way I was drawn to, even incendiary a little bit, in a way I think is healthy.'

KATE HUDSON
ERICA

'I was actually not going to be able to do the movie because I got pregnant. I just had the baby eight weeks before I started shooting. I was breastfeeding all the time, every three hours or so, and Mira would rub my feet while they were changing the set-ups. It was definitively an emotional experience for me.'

MEESHA SHAFI
BINA

'As someone who was born and raised in Lahore, I can definitively say that everyday life is very different from the footage shown in the media. And that's what this film tries to foreground.'

NEVER HIT

JIM CROSS

'Jim is someone with a job to do. He is very pragmatic and straightforward about that. It is a story about how through our own fear—and I guess our own ignorance on some level—we have taken some of our greatest allies and turned them into enemies.'

'In a way, the substance and the form of the film are very closely linked. It is a collaborative effort of people from all over the world, coming together to create this artistic vision. The film believes in the possibility of that connection and expresses it by respecting the differences of the characters.'
MOHSIN HAMID

Lunatics hijack planes in three
different states, killing thousands
of people, not to mention themselves.
It's beyond human comprehension.
How does that happen?
How does it happen like that?

What makes you think I'd know?

Agent Ford,
I love the United States of America.

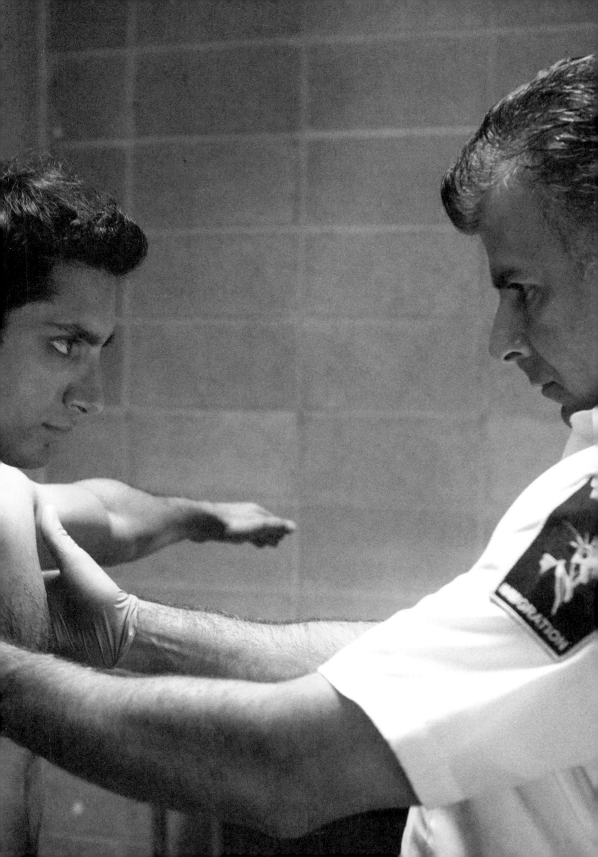

'An Indian director making a film about a Pakistani man.
That's not an easy thing to do.'
MOHSIN HAMID

FILMING

MIRA NAIR

DIRECTOR

The great beauty of making films is that cinema encompasses any inspiration: paintings, music, performance, the life around you. At the start of each film, I prepare a pretentiously titled Manifesto: a binder of references, images, colours, lines of dialogue. My visual influences for *The Reluctant Fundamentalist* were vast and eclectic—from the muted colours of the great painter Amrita Shergil to the graphic geometry of urban landscapes photographed by Andreas Gursky to the avant-garde architectural vision of my dear friends Liz Diller and Ric Scofidio. I was interested in creating a visual language for the phenomenon of globalization, which forces the energy of order and chaos to be viewed in the same frame.

The world is a complicated place. I wanted to take joy in the differences, to love them and not compromise them.

The Reluctant Fundamentalist is, in fact, an exercise in personal healing and reconnection. There are elements of me and my own family that have felt impacted by the events of the past decade. The film is an attempt, among other things, to knit the pieces back together—not by denying the tensions that have appeared, but by illustrating the ways in which we can navigate them and be human despite them.

Nothing is completely what it seems—this is a sense that permeates every aspect of my film, from the characters' divided selves to the shooting locations, in which we see Atlanta standing in for New York and Delhi substituting for Lahore and Istanbul. Everywhere we filmed, people who joined the crew and became part of the team did so because they felt this was a rare opportunity to be part of a film with a strong vision and the potential to break new ground.

Atlanta is a pretty cool city. We found the reflective-glass-and-concrete jungle of New York's financial district, authentic grunge bars to stand in for the East Village and very Williamsburg-like sections for Erica's world. Filming began here and then moved to New York for five days of exterior work.

The production then moved to Delhi for two months, where I worked with many of the crew from *Salaam Bombay!*, my 1988 debut film. Lydia and I had initially wanted to shoot in Lahore, which is very similar to the Delhi of fifty years ago. However, we were unable to get insurance to film with our US cast and crew in Pakistan, so we focused on recreating Lahore in Old Delhi, which shares a lot of cultural and architectural heritage with Lahore. We were also able to hire a production company in Lahore who shot second-unit images as per detailed conversations with me and Declan Quinn (an ace cinematographer with whom I've collaborated since 1995), and that film was processed in Bangkok.

This arrangement allowed for all of the exterior scenes of Lahore to be filmed on location in the Pakistani city, including the exuberant scenes of the city's iconic canal. And creating Lahore in Delhi was not very difficult. We found this gem of a place called the Anglo-Arabic Islamic School right in the heart of Old Delhi which dates back to the sixteenth century.

We populated this space with the detail of Lahore—from the rickshaws to the costumes to the political posters. As it is a Muslim area of Delhi, many locals were employed as extras. Spiritually it's the same as Lahore—it's not like shooting Palestine in Morocco. Some of my actors found this setting very useful, especially the proximity to the crowds and the noise of the city.

There is a palpable air of unease in every scene—a sense that anything can happen at any moment. We tried to capture that tension in the way we conceived the shots. The camera is never on a tripod in this film. It is never static. It is always moving, either in Declan's skilful hands or suspended on a bungee-cord. The camera has the breath of life in it. Declan and I both tried to find a language, something that represented that unpredictability, that tightrope. The audience is never sure of where Changez will be at the end of the story. The core for me is that this is a coming-of-age story of a young man who strives to find himself. It's a universal journey.

Istanbul, the site of Changez's personal and emotional reawakening, was also reconstituted in Delhi. All of the Turkish interiors were shot in a crumbling Delhi mansion in just one day. Two days of filming Istanbul's exteriors wrapped the entire shoot.

As on all of my films, I started each day with a yoga session with the cast and crew, using Iyengar Yoga teachers from around the world. It was a merry band. My subtitle was 'poor but free'!

MICHAEL CARLIN

PRODUCTION DESIGNER

I was working on a Fela Kuti project with Lydia Pilcher and Steve McQueen, which wasn't going ahead immediately, and Lydia suggested I might want to meet Mira and talk about the possibility of working together on William Wheeler's adaptation of *The Reluctant Fundamentalist*. I loved the novel and love Mira's films so we got together on Skype.

We bonded over our shared experiences of Kampala where Mira lives part of the time and where I had an exciting few months making *The Last King of Scotland* and I was soon on the plane to New York. The film presented some interesting challenges; the biggest was probably providing an environment for the exterior teahouse scenes that nominally take place between Anarkali Market and the university campus in Lahore. Having a main unit shooting in Lahore was deemed impossible and Mira had decided to make the Pakistani section of the film in her home city of Delhi. The streets of Old Delhi share a common architectural heritage with Lahore and Lutyen's Delhi would provide the crumbling upper middle class environment for Changez's family home.

My initial instinct was to adapt a street in Old Delhi itself, but this was the instinct of someone who had not worked in India. The volume of traffic of all kinds, the anticipated huge crowds of potential onlookers and passersby to manage and the subject matter of the film (we wanted to stage a riot)—not to mention the Indian talent for negotiation—all pointed towards a built set in a contained environment. So far so good, but the search for such a place was far from easy. I was anxious that this crucial section of the film not take place in a purely built space and that, if possible, we should benefit from some of the Islamic architecture all around us, but Old Delhi is a busy crowded place and real estate is at a premium, making it seem an impossibility When we thought we had exhausted every option, prop master Sunil Chaba suggested an old campus by Ajmeri Gate where he had filmed a scene for Richard Attenborough's *Gandhi* many years before. 'It may still be there!' he said.

An oasis of relative calm, it did house a large population of lively teenage boys after all, hiding behind high walls. Sandwiched between the railway yards, the red light district and Ajmeri Gate sits the Anglo-Arabic Islamic School. It occupies the site of an old Mughal palace and houses a beautiful red sandstone mosque from the late Mughal period. Here in the heart of Old Delhi we could build our street for the exterior teahouse and utilize the skyline of Old Delhi to stand in for Lahore. Even better, by lining up our set next to the school gates we could connect our 'back lot' set to the hectic junction of Ajmeri Gate and connect it to the 'real' world outside.

Ravi Tatva and his team of craftsmen from Mumbai and an army of local tradesmen went to work and, forty-five days later, the street was built.

DECLAN QUINN

CINEMATOGRAPHER

In discussing the visual palette early on, we tapped into Changez's view of the world: a man who 'comes from the blood of princes', whose family is in economic crisis and whose country also is in crisis. Gifted with mathematical genius, he believes America will provide the higher education and lucrative career to which he is entitled. In the early US scenes we wanted to create an illusion of power and opportunity by shooting in crisp sunlight with clear blue skies; we decided to look at Wall Street from that sleek, glass-and-steel, high-rise perspective. By contrast, the light in Lahore is filtered through dust and trees. We feel a continuity of life and tradition here that is ancient. We enter mosques and schools; we pass by remnants of colonial architecture mixed with the more austere rebar and concrete of contemporary buildings. The Lahore canal is teeming with swimming children and water buffaloes. This is the world Changez has left behind.

When Changez falls in love with Erica, the big boss's daughter, we bring in another aspect of light: flaring light. Erica is an artist who uses projectors and light boxes to display her images. This helped motivate the idea of a lens flare. I have an old lens from the seventies that reacts really beautifully to direct light hitting straight down the barrel. It creates a flare that has many facets and colours and makes my heart jump a little every time I see it. If I am operating the camera, handheld, I can move around quietly and decide when to bring the flare into the lens and when to clear it. Listening to the performance I can try to accentuate certain moments with a lens flare. To me it can feel like the 'truth' making itself present when you get that ping of vibrating light. There is a sequence in Erica's bed, a montage of intimacy between the lovers, where it works well. Later in the story, when Changez and Erica fall out at her art opening, we use the same lens-flare technique. This time slide projectors from multiple directions flare on and off, bringing complex layers of text and image together. Again, I am hoping that the effect is to underscore Changez's emotional state—in this case a sudden sense of betrayal.

Due to tax credits and financial incentives in various states and countries we are often asked to stand one location in for another. In *The Reluctant Fundamentalist,* apart from a small amount of exterior New York City, some great second-unit location in Lahore, the Atlanta Cable Company and the exteriors of Istanbul, we were faking our locations. Atlanta, Georgia stood in for New York City. New Delhi stood in for much of Lahore, Pakistan, the Philippines and the Turkish publisher interiors. Mira made a trip to Lahore in early 2011 and took a lot of lovely photos capturing the look and feel of the place. She put together a 'Look Book' which was very helpful to designer Michael Carlin and me during the pre-production phase. Michael scouted extensively around Delhi to find a place to set the teahouse, the key set of the film. There were many requirements that had to be met by this location choice: it had to be close to the university, controllable enough to stage a riot in front of and quiet enough to shoot sync sound. Michael found the Anglo-Arabic School near Ajmeri Gate in the old part of Delhi. It gave us our university exterior and the adjacent space to build a teahouse facade and market square. Michael and his crew built a beautiful teahouse that blended in with the real city just outside the gate and faced the existing Anglo-Arabic School structure which gave us the look of an old university.

We found the perfect place for the interior of the teahouse in an old low-budget hotel in the old city of Delhi. It had the patina we were searching for. Tobacco-stained walls and ceilings, fading ceramic tiles, an open atrium, a second floor balcony to give us lots of perspectives up and down and places for the actors to go. It had an old sheet metal roof that Gaffer Mulchand Dedhia and Key Grip Sanjay Sami removed. They created a truss rig from which to hang bungee for the camera and diffusion material for lighting.

The central dialogue of the film, between Changez and Bobby, occurs in various parts of the teahouse. There were big chunks of dialogue to film everyday and we needed to keep the camera fluid but not distracting for these scenes. Most of the conversation was with the actors sitting and I needed the camera to be near eye-level on the actors in order to see into their eyes. The height and open plan of the teahouse worked to our advantage. Sanjay Sami strung a thirty-foot-long piece of elastic tubing (the bungee) from a span of truss on the roof. We attached the camera and were able to float it around the actors, nearly weightless, giving me a lot of subtle control of height and position of the camera.

Istanbul was a beautiful city to set the publisher scene—a real blend of European and Muslim culture in an ancient city. We went to shoot just two days of exteriors at the end of our shooting schedule. It opened up the visual palette in an unexpected way. When Changez goes to Turkey in the story, 9/11 has happened, Changez is confused about his American life and now his ethics are challenged by someone from his own culture. It is his 'dark night' set against the blue hues of the Bosphorus and the golden domes of mosques. The crisp late sunlight in this city invoked a melancholy that illuminated Changez's dilemma.

ARJUN BHASIN

COSTUME DESIGNER

We made a lot of things. All the Pakistani clothing was made here in Delhi by tailors. We were determined to retain a sense of authenticity in the clothing. Most people often assume that there is not much difference between sartorial fashions of Delhi and Lahore. But that is not the case at all. Since there are very specific differences to Indian clothing, we couldn't go out and buy things. We made them and then added more modern contemporary elements for the students—the sort of things they would buy on the street, the kind of things they would have access to.

The interesting thing about this part of the world—whether Delhi or Lahore—is that there is a rich mix of Western clothing that is easy and modern. And yet there's also this very underlying sense of tradition. Clothing fashions are moulded out of the constant interplay of these two strong cultural influences. And that's what we sought to capture in the costumes we designed for this film.

KRIS EVANS

MAKEUP ARTIST

There are five looks on Riz. There are three beards, but five looks, and it's really important to the storyline because it's a dimension that reflects his way of deciding where he is in his life. It's important for his progression. It's not about the beard per se—it always scares me if it becomes the focal point in the movie, instead of just watching the movie and watching the character unfold. We see how the beard changes him and his dress, the way he looks, the way he behaves, his mannerisms, his speech, but everything goes together seamlessly. I always hope my makeup disappears and no one really sees it. If they're commenting about my work I'm a little nervous because I want them to forget and just watch the movie.

The challenge is that films are never shot in sequence. That's the dilemma of film-making; you always wish they would start at the beginning and just shoot through in continuity so you wouldn't have to think about it. But that's a perfect world and unfortunately even in film-making the perfect worlds go by the wayside. So you just have to adapt and keep good breakdowns with notes and photographs, so the beard growth progresses authentically, even when the scenes are being shot out of chronological order.

Earlier in the story Changez is clean-shaven but there's a little more makeup under the eyes. We made him look younger, fresher, more charismatic, happy, excited. He's accepted into a school so he's so excited about the business and the challenges, and then as he starts to get into it deeper and he realizes something's not right, maybe it's not really who he is. Then things happen within his face, colouring, under the eyes, very subtle changes, things aside from the beard. And then of course 2011 is 10 years later. So we have to show 10 years of where he's been, what he's done, and how he's thought.

Because we shot digitally, sometimes the camera is unforgiving and everything has to be very subtle. Colour has to be very simple, but the makeup supports the way he holds himself, the way he speaks, the colour of the clothes he wears, the way his hair changes. Everything about him has demeanour, a characteristic of what he's going through—as we have in real life. We change throughout our lives, and how we change! Hopefully that will also evident in the movie.

MOHSIN HAMID

NOVELIST AND SCREEN STORY WRITER

12 November 2011

My sister Nissa and I arrive in Delhi Airport. There was a time when being in Delhi Airport was a lot like being in Lahore Airport or Karachi Airport. No longer. The new version is impressive and efficient and ultra-modern and tasteful. ('Our fast bowlers are still a hell of a lot better,' I console myself, 'even the ones who aren't in jail.') Nissa and I exchange a glance at customs. Our suitcases are packed with props to make a Delhi film set look like a real Lahori street: posters, flags, fliers. We have a copy of a letter granting government permission to film in Delhi. But we don't relish the idea of explaining to an Indian customs officer why we, a pair of Pakistanis, are bringing in a bunch of political-looking banners in Urdu. Luckily no-one opens our bags. I turn on my phone and get an email from an Indian friend who says the local press is full of stories about the movie. She sends a photo of a newspaper as an attachment. There are pictures of Mira Nair (the director), Riz Ahmed (the lead actor), and Meesha Shafi (who plays Riz's sister, and who will be flying back to Lahore in a couple hours on the same plane that brought us in). As for the 'exclusive' details about the film exposed in the article, well, they're mostly pretty far off. There is, for example, no 'border-crossing-into-India scene' and Om Puri's character isn't 'a village thakur'. At least I hope not. Better get my hands on a copy of the latest script fast.

13 November 2011

After a lovely dinner with Mira and other people from the film (at which it's confirmed that no India-border-crossings or village thakurs have slipped into the script), followed by a lengthy exploration of Delhi nightlife, I wake up well-rested and ready to go. Too well-rested. I've slept past the shoot's 6 a.m. start time by three hours. Rush to the set in panic. Luckily no-one seems surprised or alarmed. They've clearly met writers before. The set itself

is a revelation. To recreate the interior of an Old Anarkali cafe, Mira has commandeered a gorgeous, seedy, atmospheric, run-down little hotel opposite the Old Delhi railway station. The crew has removed the roof and replaced it with transparent plastic. Declan Quinn, the director of photography (who has shot *Leaving Las Vegas*, *28 Days*, *Monsoon Wedding* and dozens of other films) is supervising the creation of elaborate screens, meshes and leaf-camouflage-nets—the kind you sometimes see on military installations—in order to make sure the light is exactly right. It finally dawns on me just how extensive film production really is, even on an independent film like this one. There are over a hundred people in the crew doing everything from rigging up bungee cables that support the camera to processing digital outputs in real time to scuffing up cafe tables with lit cigarettes to making sure every actor's wrist-watch shows the same time. Any belief I might have had that I could easily segue into doing what Mira does vanishes. Yes, being a director has similarities to being a novelist: both have to tell a story. But for me a day's work is like entering a quiet, sheltered, unhurried cocoon. For a director it's like talking on three different cell phones while riding a unicycle on the wing of an airplane in heavy turbulence.

14 November 2011

Early call from Lydia Pilcher, the film's producer. She wants me to attend an impromptu script rewriting session in Liev Schreiber's hotel suite before today's shooting. Liev (he's been Hamlet, Henry V and Macbeth, but here in Delhi people excitedly yell out 'Sabretooth' as he walks by because of his role in an X-men film) plays the American character Riz meets and tells his story to. In my book, that character has no name and no lines. In the film, he has a name, and he has lines, and some of those lines are about to change. Bill Wheeler, the Los Angeles-based writer who did the most recent drafts of the screenplay, isn't in India, so I gather with Mira, Lydia, Riz, Liev and Ami Boghani (associate producer and co-writer) to do some revisions over breakfast. Discussions are had. Lines are tweaked. Discussions are had. Lines are tweaked. Discussions are had... Filming is pushed back. We eat lunch and keep working, except for Riz who has to go into makeup. His beard takes two hours to apply: it's done hair by hair. He must be thanking the heavens this isn't Planet of the Apes. When filming can't be delayed any further, we stop rewriting and screech off through packed Delhi traffic to the set. Nissa has been there all morning, giving advice on making things look as Lahori as possible. She fills me in on what's been going on. Then filming starts. In between takes we look at some of the lines again. Movies are about constant readjustments, it seems. Novel to script. Script to revised script. Revised script to shooting script. Shooting script to what the actors actually say. What the actors actually say to what gets edited into the film. And so on. But for now it's phones off, lights on, beard-hairs poised, and... action. Three days in Delhi down. Two more weeks to go.

'The film is not a condemnation of either Pakistan or America.
It shows the world as a complicated place, where centrifugal forces
are trying to push the world apart. By humanizing the characters,
we are attempting to bring the world back together.'
MOHSIN HAMID

Your father was a poet?
You should be ashamed of yourself,
doing what you're doing here.

I don't want this
kingdom, Lord
All I want is a
grain of respect.

You picked a side
after 9/11.
I didn't have to.
It was picked
for me.

                        CHANGEZ
            Oh, Agent Ford, I just *love* the
            United States of America.

INT. CHANGEZ'S APARTMENT - NIGHT

Changez sits facing the window, in the dark. His phone rings
and he lets it go to voicemail.

                        ERICA (O.S.)
            Honey, I can't wait to see you at
            my opening tonight. Corner of
            Crosby and Prince. See you...

EXT. NEW YORK CITY STREET, 2001 - DUSK

It is dark in downtown Manhattan. Changez walks through the
streets and spots a pack of hipsters lingering outside an
unnamed building. Changez rushes inside.

INT. GALLERY X, NYC - EVENING

He walks into the dark, smoky space. Black and white images
and text are projected onto large sheets. Chalk outlines
made from neon lights trickle down the brick walls, like
bodies falling from the sky. Changez suddenly realizes that
he is surrounded by images of himself. There, in the middle
of the gallery, are displayed the words, *"PRETEND I'M HIM."*
Flashes of text like, "Throw a Burqa on me" and "I had a
Pakistani once". Erica takes a moment from soaking up
praise.

                        ERICA
            Changez!   I'm so happy you're
            here.

Suddenly aware of being recognized - Changez feels the eyes
of the room upon him.

                        CHANGEZ
            What have you done?

Erica is immediately alarmed.

                        ERICA
            What do you mean? This is us. It's
            about us.

                        CHANGEZ
            From you too now?

His voice rises.

CONFORMED SCRIPT - MAY.11.12 71.

                    CHANGEZ (CONT'D)
          The one person in the whole goddam
          city I trusted - and I get this
          shit, this fucking shit from you
          too?

                    ERICA
          I thought you'd be proud of me?

                    CHANGEZ
          Why would I be proud? Proud of
          what, being your little pet
          artistic project?

The patrons notice the argument between artist and subject.
Some watch it voyeuristically, thinking it might be part of
the show.

                    ERICA
          Can we take this outside, please...

                    CHANGEZ
          Was that the idea? How chic! I'll
          date a Pakistani two months after
          9/11! Good for your bohemian
          street cred, right?

                    ERICA
          That's completely unfair.

                    CHANGEZ
          "I fucked the twentieth hijacker" -
          I'm like the ultimate downtown
          status symbol!

Erica has started crying. She flees into the back hallway of
the gallery.

INT. GALLERY HALLWAY - NIGHT

 Changez charges after her.

                    CHANGEZ
          That's it? You're just going to
          walk away?

                    ERICA
          And your feelings are all pure?
          Would you have been interested in
          me if my uncle wasn't your CEO? If
          my mother lived in Queens instead
          of Park and 85th?

                    CHANGEZ
          You've got to be kidding me. You're
          a sick girl. It was never about
          that for me.

EDITING

SHIMIT AMIN

EDITOR

The entirety of the film's post-production took place in India, with the edit happening in Delhi and Bombay.

We tried to edit simultaneously while Mira was shooting, and show her what we'd done on her days off. We had to do it this way, to build the story day by day as the film was being shot.

There are so many layers in this movie; it's like a cat-and-mouse game. Yes, it's a thriller, but it has this whole world of Lahore, Pakistan, in it—that's the flavor we're trying to get out of it, a world that hasn't been seen. This is actually a very human thriller. Unlike cold and distant thrillers, you feel for these characters. That's what Mira has shot and worked towards with the actors, and that's what we carried forward in the editing.

When I read the script, I realized the kind of voice within it has never been heard on an international scale. It's a vision and a voice from this part of the world that has never been expressed, and one which we are trying to get across to people who don't usually pay attention to it at all.

Our key aim is to tell a great story that's really well-written, has incredible layers to it, has business, romance, a whole political angle—and then we're trying to combine that with the storyline of Changez's family. And once we put that together, we had to worry about balancing it. But that's the fun part, how all of these things mix in.

The introduction to the film is so important, and I always knew that we would really have to nail that opening sequence with the qawwali singers.

MIRA NAIR IN CONVERSATION WITH SHIMIT AMIN
ON THE EDITING OF THE QAWWALI SEQUENCE OF THE FILM

S: While I was editing the film—and I think this was in our later edited sequences, because this is India—I remember thinking, 'Well, I have to deal with this sequence, it's a huge sequence and it's the beginning of the film and I don't wanna screw it up.' So I digested the footage for a long time, I kept watching it, watching it, watching it. I remember sitting with you and going through all the qawwali stuff, and discussing all the wonderful footage that had been shot. I remember both of us making remarks like 'I love this', 'I love that', 'I love these shots'. One thing that we always saw and we agreed about simultaneously was that shot of Changez's that ended up in the beginning of the film. I remember that being really vivid to both of us—we said, almost together, 'This has to be the first shot of the film' while we watched the footage.

M: Yes, because he had about him an enigma and a beauty and it was just a quiet, mysterious kind of beginning.

S: Yes. Absolutely. And you know we had to, of course, start with our protagonist Changez, so, in that scene, the most beautiful frame set him up with mystery, as you said. You know that there is mystery behind who this person is. We had those shots, we viewed the qawwali and it was very impressive in the way you had shot it. You and Declan had just approached the thing, the whole coverage of it and moving the camera and the qawwals who weren't performing— they were performers, but they weren't necessarily, I would say, lip-syncers. Qawwali is a very improvised art—you just plug into a performance and you just follow that. So there, the singers —not in a bad way—had difficulty following what they had sung, because no two qawwali performances are the same. They weren't used to following something, repeating it, take after take. That was something that we observed in the editing room, and we began to worry about how we would be able to edit the takes because they had different—however slightly—rhythms every single time. Everyone, I remember, was worried about how to make that flow, and I think that it all came together because we had lots of nice pieces. I think the qawwali was originally fourteen minutes.

M: It was a sixteen-minute qawwali originally in the music, and then we cut it down to eight minutes in the editing room as a piece of sound, and then we shot those eight minutes in fluidity. But for me, what informed the script from the very beginning was for the first shot to open on a regular Lahore evening; of course, an upper-middle-class Lahore evening, where it is quite the norm to have a singer or singers come and speak in song for a family. It's just an incredibly divine sort of feeling when you're there. I wanted to evoke that, but we needed to

Shot breakdown

#3: Family Home / Singers

- Servants putting on fire torchlight in garden - increase sense of
- danger. Ch. passes fire en route car - enters the darkness of living room as he exits.
- Camera intros to the family ma distracted by phone call
- detail of phone in his hand
- details of singers' hands in song linking us to Ch. passing them
- CU of paan-stained mouth of singer
-

create a context for why Bobby and Changez are meeting in the tea house in the consequent scene. In the book, it is very easy to assume that they just meet in the tea house but in a movie you have to show why they met. And from the very beginning—I mean as far back as I can remember when we were thinking of this film—I remember telling all the writers that this is how it has to begin: the intercutting of the qawwali with the kidnapping. What I always loved about Farid Iyaz [one of the qawwali singers] especially was his paan-stained teeth—throughout the shooting I kept on feeding him more paan, because the red of the paan was going to evoke the blood of the kidnapping and we—quite literally, since the camera was on a bungee—would enter his mouth at certain moments of the performance.

S: I remember, to add to your idea of the paan, that you also had him do hand gestures that were kind of evocative of the violence that would take place on the other side of town. I thought it was wonderful that you married those two things together—there is something happening in the other part of the town but the hand gestures are kind of telling you what it is, what you might expect, just hinting at it.

M: Evocative of the 'lapak jhapak', the fact that everything could go upside down.

S: And also at that one point where Abu just thrusts his hand forward and the woman falls on the other side of town—that was very interesting; you let the hands kind of portray the violence.

M: Hands and the words. But it was all your cutting that actually linked the gesture of the hands being thrown towards the camera with the kidnapping and the woman being thrown on the road. I remember the first time—your cut was about almost nine minutes, and it was so beautifully cut that it was impossible to unravel that for a while. We sat on it, although I knew it would be too long.

S: Yes, I think we both knew that it was long, but we wanted to see fully the execution of our original intention, to see how the song had gone into play and how the events were happening. It was like a step that we took, saying that we must see what this looks like and, you know, I felt it was wonderful. If you just see that footage before it was edited, you really get this sense of what a qawwali experience is! It is intoxication and, you know, I feel that song that you'd picked just completely embodies that kind of a feeling. And the performers as well.

M: I mean, they walked across the border from Lahore to be in that scene! They came from Karachi.

S: I remember you telling me. And it's amazing, amazing!

M: And it's this whole family, from nephew to grandpa, the whole twelve members of the

Sufi / Pakistan
Qawwali
Farid Ayaz + family
"Chaap Tilak"
abject surrender

Dawn
Daily Times
Express editorials
    tribune

tribune.com.pk

Standing f Am values
does not make an American ally
Am not true to its own values
Am doesn't stand f these
Trump anymore

family. But I remember Liev and Naomi arriving that night from America while the qawwali was going on, and it became this spontaneous party after we finished shooting, where they just sang for us right through till the moon came up. It was an extraordinary evening.

S: The closest thing I can say is jazz—in a way, you cannot put a structure to this kind of music. Jazz, with a Sufi-jazz kind of a tone, and I feel it comes through for the audience, because everybody reacts to it when you watch it. But having to portray that in the editing was very crucial. Just to get the performance in was very, very crucial, because Declan's just so good at capturing music. You know he is a very fantastic photographer of music, and he did that wonderfully. His shooting of it was superb; with him on board there's always a sense of a little bit of pressure, like, let's hope the performance really lives up to that, to his kind of wonderful, you know. Watching that scene, the audience should feel like, yes, there's a story that we have to really attend to, but then, let's also enjoy this performance. Acha, this is an experience for the film.

M: Yes, it's not about the detail, about what you call ooodh being taken, or you know, the gajra ke phool. It was an introduction to each member of the family.

S: And the introduction to a culture in a very incredible way.

M: In a very ordinary way. There were a lot of things that play with the camera. Declan was on the bungee and moving, but Shankar Raman, our second cinematographer, was just moving with long lenses, laterally throughout the performance, so we always had this mixture of the fluid camera and moving-but-still camera.

S: What were your instructions to the actors who were part of this? I was always curious of what you told them, because it wasn't really that scripted.

M: The camera was always fluid, so you never know when actors were on screen. But I would just tell them to basically get lost in the music and to sit straight and the details, you know, spell out the characters. Beena attended to the uncle in his gas mask and, of course, to the parents the minute Changez gets the phone call. It's all sort of set-up, like bit of a red herring, where he gets the phone call and we follow him behind the reeds and you think he's involved with the kidnapping and the parents perk up. So it was the drama of the piece that I outlined. They had to simply play their parts and our camera would find them—they were never set up like 'Okay, yeh aapka shot hai' kind of thing. The camera would find Om and Shabana and this and that.

S: It's highly irregular in film shooting. You were giving them the ambience in which to play their parts, and you just captured it all. Which is wonderful, and which I always love when you break away from the film-making.

M: Yes, and occasionally I would throw out commands from behind the camera: now Shabana come and sit up front, and all of that. We did a lot of work with sound as well.

S: I remember you giving specific dialogues to Om about what he needed to say, and that was something that I feel is unique for the Western audience. With Indian or South Asian classical music, there is an interaction between the audience and the performers, which is unnerving to a lot of Western viewers, audiences, listeners. And I feel that interaction is such a crucial part, even if it's jarring for Western audiences. But Om Puri talking in the middle of a performance is normal in our part of the world, which is wonderful.

M: I just asked Ali Sethi, a wonderful Pakistani poet and a young friend who was with us throughout the shoot, 'What would he, what could he say?' He said, 'Yaar, the last concert I was at this guy, uncle or maybe somebody, said, "Maar ditta yaar. Ainj bhi marna hai, onj bhi marna hai", which is basically, "He is killing me, the music is killing me; if you gotta die anyway, you might as well die in this kinda thing, listening." It's a kind of Punjabi concept of living life fully and big.' And that, in one line, is the philosophy of the family in a way. Om is such an authentic actor that he just nailed it. And so that's where it comes from. It comes from observations really, from these mehfils night after night that I used to go to in Lahore. We used to have them in India, too—we still do—but in Pakistan it seems to be a way of life, amongst the upper middle class, at least. Live music is just available.

S: And it's not rude to interact with the performer. Something very similar happens in jazz actually.

M: In fact, the performers would be really upset if you didn't interact, if you didn't respond verbally.

S: Which is that 'Wah wah!' Which is typical, as part of the culture and the tradition of music like this. Hopefully, people get that. In the editing, it's very important to understand that, and it may not be something everyone is used to. We had to make sure that it all feels natural, because we wouldn't want to have to stop and explain that.

M: No no no no. It's just the way it is. It's just the way it is.

'This story gave me the chance to let people see beyond that terrible stereotype that is constantly projected in our texts and media: if you're a Muslim you're a terrorist, if you're an American you're a militarist . . . So much is ignorance, so much is insularity. So much is just plain short-sightedness.'

MIRA NAIR

You say things to burn the heart,
You speak of a nest now broken.

You inflict such suffering.
Yet say I must smile.

MUSIC

Mori Araj Suno
Faiz Ahmed Faiz

Hear me out, O Lord

It was You, true Lord, who said

'Man, you are king of the world.'

My bounties are all for you benefit

My viceroy and of exalted rank are you

A fine king you made, O Lord!

. . . who endures life's blows with grace

I don't want this kingdom, Lord!

All I want is a grain of respect

Hear me out, O Lord!

Heed my plea, and I'll heed Yours

Curse me, if I break this vow

If this pact displeases You,

Then let me go find another God

Faiz Ahmed Faiz (1911–84) was a revolutionary poet often punished for his views.
A Marxist who transcended religious divisions, he was one of the great masters of
Urdu poetry and a towering Pakistani intellectual.

موری ارج سنو

موری ارج سنو دست گیر پیر

ربّا سچّیا توں تے آکھیا سی

جا اوئے بندیا جک دا شاہ ہیں توں

سائیاں نعمتاں تیریاں دولتاں نیں

ساڈا نیب تے عالیجاہ ہیں توں

چنگا شاہ بنایا ای ربّ سائیاں

پولے کھاندے وار نہ آوندی اے

مینوں شاہی نئیں چاہیدی ربّ میرے

میں تے عزت دا تکّر منگناں ہاں

موری ارج سنو دست گیر پیر

میری منّیں تے تیریاں میں منّاں

تیری سونہہ جے اک وی گلّ موڑاں

جے ایہہ سودا نیئں پجدا تیں ربّا

فیر میں جاواں تے ربّ کوئی ہور لوڑاں

THE
RELUCTANT
FUNDAMENTALIST

MIRA NAIR

DIRECTOR

Music is a huge part of my breathing universe. Sometimes it is a piece of music that first draws me into a film. In this case, it was two songs: 'Mori Araj Suno', the Tina Sani version; and the great qawwali 'Kangna', sung by Fareed Ayaz and Abu Mohammed, which features as the first seven minutes of the film. Both were produced by the contemporary music programme in Pakistan, *Coke Studio*. Ali Sethi and Mehreen Jabbar introduced me to this modern sound, sending me the latest songs that melded together legendary singers and younger musicians to re-imagine ancient songs with jazz and folk influences. At the core of this movement is a remarkable music maker, Rohail Hyatt, whom I went to meet in Karachi. He had become very successful setting up this programme all over the subcontinent, so he couldn't compose for my film. However, he remained a brother throughout the journey that resulted in the hybrid sound of *The Reluctant Fundamentalist*.

I was confident about exploring the subcontinental sound of the film, but needed a film composer who would understand the American heartbeat—because whatever else this film may be, it's equally about the dream of America: people falling in love with it, people falling out of love with it. In the 'temp' scoring of the film, Shimit and I found ourselves turning to *Donnie Darko*, the cult film of the '90s—and so I called its iconoclastic composer, Mike Andrews, in California. We didn't waste time and were very direct, plunging into a conversation that spanned the universe. I asked him how far east he had travelled and he said, 'San Diego!' I just started laughing. Next thing, he was on a plane to Delhi.

As we edited the film, I knew I wanted a young, male, rough voice to express the spirit of Changez in song. I turned to the same words that had kept me going through the ups and downs of the incredibly difficult journey it was to make this film: Faiz's great poem, 'Mori Araj Suno'. I went back to Pakistan and found Atif Aslam, the nation's biggest pop star. He created a new melody for 'Mori Araj Suno', which we then sent to Mike in LA to create the overlay of contemporary funk. The song became the call to action as Changez quits his job and sails down the Bosphorus in Istanbul, the turning point of our story.

The great privilege of being a director is that one can include the voices with which you fall in love. I had fallen in love with Lahore, with the largesse of live music that I heard virtually every night in people's living rooms. I heard Zahra Khan (our novelist Mohsin Hamid's wife) sing one night and was amazed by her full-bodied voice, earthy and sensual, like a modern-day Reshma. She had to be in the film—and so she came into the studio, eight months' pregnant and breathless, to perform the Punjabi folk song 'Kaindey Ney Naina' acapella. And a week later, Mike Andrews in California added his heavenly slide guitar to make a sublime song in the wedding scene of the film.

We were blessed with having Meesha Shafi, one of the great songstresses of Pakistan, make her cinematic debut in the film playing Changez's sister Bina. Who hasn't fallen for Meesha in her fantastic rendition of 'Chori Chori' or 'Jugni' in *Coke Studio*? So we had her sing her own song 'Bijli' in the dholki scene—and as I filmed her, I found myself asking: how can so much talent and beauty and sparkle exist in one human being?

Of course it was Junior Masterji, Ali Sethi (my teacher in singing), who opened so many doors to the music in this film. As an undergraduate at Harvard, he belted out Farida Khanum's 'Aaj Jaaney Ki Zid Na Karo' for me, ultimately inviting me for my first trip to Pakistan in 2004—and beginning the whole journey that resulted in this film being made. We recorded Ali singing 'Dil Jalaaney Ki Baat' on the stage of the moth-eaten Ritz theatre in Ajmeri Gate. We used his beautiful voice, unfettered, at the end of the wedding scene when Changez humiliates his father.

Faiz's classic poem, 'Bol', was another cornerstone of inspiration throughout. Shabana had sung a beautiful version of it during our rehearsals, but I wanted a modern version that intertwined Urdu and English, so that young people across the world could know the power of his words that urge one 'to speak, to say what you have to say'. For this I turned to an old friend— the great guru of rock, Peter Gabriel—who had first brought the unforgettable Ustad Nusrat Fateh Ali Khan to the world stage. I had practically stalked Peter after his classic soundtrack for Scorsese's *The Last Temptation of Christ*, and although we didn't make music together over the years, we became friends in our shared activism. I sent Peter forty minutes of the film and he was hooked. He offered to compose one original song—'Bol'—for the end credits of the film, with the Urdu sung by Atif Aslam. With all of us working on this song—Peter in London, Atif in Lahore, me in Kampala—it's been a crazy, beautiful journey, and dream come true in front of my eyes and ears: Peter and Atif's haunting voices carrying the power of Faiz's words across the world.

Music, as we know, knows no borders.

MICHAEL ANDREWS

COMPOSER

'Hello Michael'

'Hello Mira . . . Mira?'

The line is dead. Well, let's try this again. Shoot, I don't know how to call India. So I wait. Ok, so I wait... a few minutes go by. It's late here in California, but twelve and half hours ahead, it's morning. Finally, the phone rings and I pick up.

'It's India, man, welcome to my world.'

I am a little nervous. This woman is one of the world's great film-makers and somehow a film score I worked on over a decade ago has made it onto her radar. She compliments my handmade approach. We begin with the basics. Who am I? Born and raised in Southern California, self-taught, son of a music teacher. I know very little about India or Pakistan.

The dialogue heads straight into comfortable territory. We both agree that it is important to stay strong and maintain a personal vision. We talk about the pitfalls of success and how important decisions of the heart are in creating films and music. Immediately we are friends. The conversation is ninety minutes long.

You got the film. But you have to go to India to meet Mira and watch the film.

Originally, I told Mira, the handmade approach she loves is a result of my being at home working in my space with all my gear and musical tools. So, of course she comes back with a request to leave home. I will come to learn that this is part of her approach. I love what you do but I want you to stretch out of your boundaries and come into mine. Go out of your comfort zone and let's see where we end up.

So within the week I am at the airport in Delhi, taking in foreign smells and the surrounding sounds of daybreak. Her gracious assistant Rahul is there to meet me, complete with a permanent laptop in his hands. This guy is on the run dealing with a woman constantly on the move physically and mentally. Eventually we end up at my guest house where I rest for a few hours before heading into the editing room, an apartment two blocks away.

I am seated in front of the computer screen in a bedroom that has been turned into an editing room. There I watch the recent cut of *The Reluctant Fundamentalist* alone, top to bottom with no music. Immediately after the viewing I emerge from the room into the light and there is Mira. Like an old friend she greeted me with a big smile and a hug. 'What did you think?' she asks. 'A lot,' I think I replied.

For the next three days we watch the movie over and over talking about each scene at length and how the music should be approached. We discuss not only music but how the movie has made its mark on me. At this point I am one of a very few people to have seen the whole thing, maybe the only Westerner. She wants the movie to build bridges, she keeps saying, and I suppose I am the other side of the bridge. As I talk about the movie she listens intently; she seems very humble. It was clear that she wanted me to contribute to the fabric of the film, with my own thread.

Before I leave to go back to America, Mira treats me to a few of her favourite spots and introduces me to her close friends, saying, I have to eat this and drink that and see this etc. I must say all her choices agreed with me. One night Mira takes me to a Sufi music festival held in an old temple all decked out with carpets covering the entire floor and the ruins lit up for dramatic effect. We make our way inside and Mira begins jockeying for better seats. Hailing over the promoter she knows—she knows everyone—she lets him know we demand better seats. She is the kind of woman that can get you a better seat anywhere anytime. This woman makes a film for one fifth of what it would cost any other film-maker.

When I return home I begin the composition process. I am searching for sounds. I play slideshows of my own photographs from Delhi combing through sense memory while I scroll through music. *The Reluctant Fundamentalist* is really a modern film in every sense and I want the score to feel modern. So I put together some almost sound collage type music, drone music. I also put a couple of pieces together that have tabla and dhol on them. I send it to Mira and honestly she is puzzled by it. After a phone call with me basically saying maybe you need another person to do this, her simple response was, 'Hey man, hold on . . . I hired you to be you, give me your perspective and just some of your melodies, your sound.'

Mira did want other instruments from Pakistan. She has great relationships with folks in the region and because I was so far away and very busy Mira actually took care of it. I sent her my music to be overdubbed with melodies represented and she actually recorded the bansuri [flute] and also took care of the vocal on 'Mori Araj Suno'. Simultaneously I added Alam Khan, Ali Akbar's son and Salar Nadir. Then I put the tracks under the vocal and the orchestra under the mock-up and real bansuri. Imagine all this over the internet, uploading and downloading. No in person interaction yet. Most of our discussions took place after she had worked a sixteen-hour day.

I will definitely never say this film was easy. But once we got our groove we began to find a common ground. Like all film scores they start as one thing and end up as another. Mostly because music is something people love to talk about and it's also something that can never be entirely understood in words. It's as simple as I make it, she hears it and either says, I like it or I don't.

After months of working Mira finally came to me at my home studio and we combed the score. She sat in the back of my studio as I played instrument after instrument, layer after layer. All the while she was remote editing over the internet with Shimit. We expanded the score to include a string group to give Mira the more expansive sound she wanted. When you work for Mira you can't help but want to do everything possible and impossible. She is so committed to her vision that all the twists and turns are part of the search for what the film is. With all the shading and framing taking place in editorial the music had to bob and weave in the process of defining the final tone. Mira wanted the whole world to be open to this film, so hopefully the music helped in that regard.

After a couple weeks of tweaking and some recording and mixing we were finally finishing up. Mira promised to cook for us, her 'actor seduction meal'. We ate and drank and enjoyed the company like a large family. We both agreed that the best films are where you work hard, reach the other side, and know that you have made a lifelong friend.

'Some financiers early on wondered if the film would still feel relevant by the time it was made. Unless world peace is imminent, the significance of these themes will never recede.'
LYDIA DEAN PILCHER

Do not cry for our son.
Too many tears have filled this river.

Do not act to avenge him.
Too much blood has poured into this river.

Do not shake your fist at fate,
for Allah Himself holds our son in His embrace

Liev Schreiber   Kate Hudson   Riz Ahmed

Shabana Azmi   Om Puri   Kiefer Sutherland

Nelsan Ellis   Martin Donovan   Haluk Bilginer

Imaad Shah   Meesha Shafi

CAST

CHANGEZ	RIZ AHMED
ERICA	KATE HUDSON
BOBBY LINCOLN	LIEV SCHREIBER
JIM CROSS	KIEFER SUTHERLAND
ABU	OM PURI
AMMI	SHABANA AZMI
LUDLOW COOPER	MARTIN DONOVAN
WAINWRIGHT	NELSAN ELLIS
NAZMI KEMAL	HALUK BILGINER
BINA	MEESHA SHAFI
SAMEER	IMAAD SHAH
MIKE RIZZO	CHRIS SMITH
JUNAID	ASHWATH BHATT
CLEA	SARAH QUINN
BANDY UNCLE	CHANDRACHUR SINGH
MUSTAFA FAZIL	ADIL HUSSAIN
AHMED	ALI SETHI
AMREH	DEEPTI DATT
ANSE RAINIER	GARY RICHARDSON
NADIA	SONIA JEHAN
RANTING SOUTH ASIAN MAN	GOLAM SARWAR HARUN
RAHIM	ROHAN GUPTA
JUNE DAVIS	CLAIRE ROBERTS LAMONT
MAXWELL UNDERWOOD	VICTOR SLEZAK

JAEGER-leCOULTRE   LANCIA

MOSTRA INT
D'ARTE CIN
la Biennale

RIZ AHMED